MOVIE VOCAL SELECTIONS

CHICAGO

D0567626

*Not in the film, but included on the soundtrack.

MIRAMAX FILMS Presents a PRODUCER CIRCLE CO. PRODUCTION

a ZADAN/MERON PRODUCTION

RENÉE ZELLWEGER   CATHERINE ZETA-JONES   AND RICHARD GERE   "CHICAGO"

QUEEN LATIFAH   JOHN C. REILLY   LUCY LIU   TAYE DIGGS   COLM FEORE   CASTING BY LAURA ROSENTHAL & ALI FARRELL   COSTUME DESIGNER COLLEEN ATWOOD   MUSIC SUPERVISOR MAUREEN CROWE   EXECUTIVE MUSIC PRODUCERS ERIC WAKE   RANDY SPENDLOVE   MUSIC SUPERVISED AND CONDUCTED BY PAUL BOGAEV

ORIGINAL SCORE MUSIC BY DANNY ELFMAN   CHOREOGRAPHED BY ROB MARSHALL   EDITED BY MARTIN WALSH   PRODUCTION DESIGNER JOHN MYHRE   DIRECTOR OF PHOTOGRAPHY DION BEEBE, ACS   CO PRODUCER DON CARMODY   BASED ON THE MUSICAL PLAY "CHICAGO"   DIRECTED AND CHOREOGRAPHED FOR THE STAGE BY BOB FOSSE

BOOK OF THE MUSICAL PLAY BY BOB FOSSE & FRED EBB   MUSIC BY JOHN KANDER   LYRICS BY FRED EBB   PRODUCED ON THE STAGE BY ROBERT FRYER   JAMES CRESSON   MARTIN RICHARDS   IN ASSOCIATION WITH JOSEPH HARRIS   IRA BERNSTEIN   LYRICS AND MUSIC PUBLISHED BY UNICHAPPELL MUSIC INC.

BASED ON THE PLAY BY MAURINE DALLAS WATKINS   EXECUTIVE PRODUCERS CRAIG ZADAN   NEIL MERON   PRODUCERS HARVEY WEINSTEIN   MERYL POSTER   JULIE GOLDSTEIN   JENNIFER BERMAN   BOB WEINSTEIN   SAM CROTHERS

SCREENPLAY BY BILL CONDON   PRODUCED BY MARTIN RICHARDS   DIRECTED BY ROB MARSHALL

PG-13 PARENTS STRONGLY CAUTIONED
Some Material May Be Inappropriate for Children Under 13
Sexual Content and Dialogue, Violence and Thematic Elements

SOUNDTRACK AVAILABLE ON   SONY MUSIC SOUNDTRAX   READ THE NEWMARKET PRESS BOOK   www.miramax.com/chicago   MIRAMAX FILMS

ISBN 0-634-05955-6

HAL•LEONARD®
CORPORATION
7777 W. BLUEMOUND RD. P.O. BOX 13819 MILWAUKEE, WI 53213

For all works contained herein:
Unauthorized copying, arranging, adapting, recording or public performance is an infringement of copyright.
Infringers are liable under the law.

Visit Hal Leonard Online at
www.halleonard.com

FILM CAST AND CREW

Directed and Choreographed by Rob Marshall
Screenplay by Bill Condon
Produced by Martin Richards

Principal Cast:

Renée Zellweger..............ROXIE HART
Catherine Zeta-Jones .....VELMA KELLY
Richard Gere....................BILLY FLYNN
John C. Reilly ....AMOS HART
Queen Latifah ....MATRON "MAMA" MORTON
Christine Baranski............MARY SUNSHINE

SYNOPSIS
of the film adaptation

Everyone loves a legend, but in Chicago, there's only room for one. Velma Kelly (CATHERINE ZETA-JONES) burns in the spotlight as a nightclub sensation. When she shoots her philandering husband, she lands on Chicago's famed murderess row, retains Chicago's slickest lawyer, Billy Flynn (RICHARD GERE), and is the center of the town's most notorious murder case, only increasing her celebrity.

Roxie Hart (RENÉE ZELLWEGER), seduced by the city's promise of style and adventure, dreams of singing and dancing her way to stardom. When Roxie's abusive lover tries to walk out on her, she too ends up in prison. Billy recognizes a made-for-tabloids story, and postpones Velma's court date to take on Roxie's case. Infamy is Roxie's ticket to stardom. Billy turns her crime of passion into celebrity headlines, and in this town, where murder is a form of entertainment, she becomes a bona fide star—much to Velma's chagrin.

As Roxie fashions herself as America's sweetheart, Velma has more than a few surprises in store, and the two women stop at nothing to outdo each other in their obsessive pursuit of fame and celebrity. A new interpretation that takes the award-winning Broadway show into fresh and expansive cinematic realms, CHICAGO shifts adroitly from the reality of intrigue, rivalry and betrayal to spectacular fantasies of music and dance, offering tongue-in-cheek commentary on the cult of celebrity and the scandalous lengths to which people will go to attain it.

CHICAGO ON STAGE

CHICAGO – A Musical Vaudeville
Music by John Kander
Lyrics by Fred Ebb
Book by Fred Ebb and Bob Fosse
Based on the 1926 play *Chicago* by Maurine Dallas Watkins

The Original Broadway Production
Directed and Choreographed by Bob Fosse
Opened June 3, 1975 at the 46th Street Theatre

Principal Original Cast:

Gwen Verndon............,,,,ROXIF HART
Chita Rivera ....VELMA KELLY
Jerry Orbach ....BILLY FLYNN
Barney Martin ....AMOS HART
Mary McCartney ....MATRON "MAMA" MORTON
M. O'Haughey ....MARY SUNSHINE

Of interest: during the run Liza Minnelli and Ann Reinking also played Roxie.

The Revival
Directed by Walter Bobbie
Choreographed by Anne Reinking (in the style of Bob Fosse)
Opened on Broadway on November 16, 1996 at the Shubert Theater

Principal New York Revival Original Cast:

Ann Reinking ....ROXIE HART
Bebe Neuwirth.............VELMA KELLY
James Naughton ....BILLY FLYNN
Joel Grey ....AMOS HART
Marcia Lewis ....MATRON "MAMA" MORTON
D. Sabella....................MARY SUNSHINE

The same production opened in London on November 18, 1997
at the Adelphi Theatre.

Principal London Original Cast:

Ruthie Henshall...........ROXIE HART
Ute Lemper.................VELMA KELLY
Henry Goodman ....BILLY FLYNN
Nigel Planer................AMOS HART
Meg Johnson..............MATRON "MAMA" MORTON
C. Shirvell....................MARY SUNSHINE

CHICAGO

AND ALL THAT JAZZ

Words by FRED EBB
Music by JOHN KANDER

Moderately slow, deliberately

Come on, babe, _ why don't we paint the town, _ And

all that jazz! _ I'm gon - na rouge my knees _ and roll my stock - ings down _

And all that jazz! _ Start the car, _ I know a whoop - ee spot _ where the

Copyright © 1973, 1975 by Unichappell Music Inc. and Kander & Ebb, Inc.
Copyright Renewed
All Rights Administered by Unichappell Music Inc.
International Copyright Secured   All Rights Reserved

ba - by's queer __ for all that jazz! _____

Find a flask, __ we're play - ing fast and loose __ and

Oh, _____ you're gon - na see your She - ba

all that jazz! __ Right up here __ is where I

shim - my shake, __ And all that jazz! __ Oh, _____

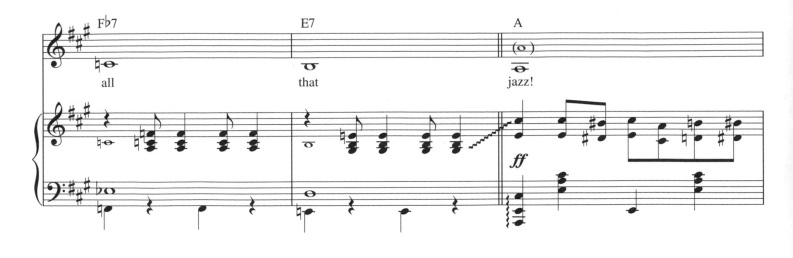

all that jazz!

FUNNY HONEY

Words by FRED EBB
Music by JOHN KANDER

* Sung an octave lower

Copyright © 1973, 1975 by Unichappell Music Inc. and Kander & Ebb, Inc.
Copyright Renewed
All Rights Administered by Unichappell Music Inc.
International Copyright Secured All Rights Reserved

That sun - ny, fun - ny, hon - ey hub - by of ___

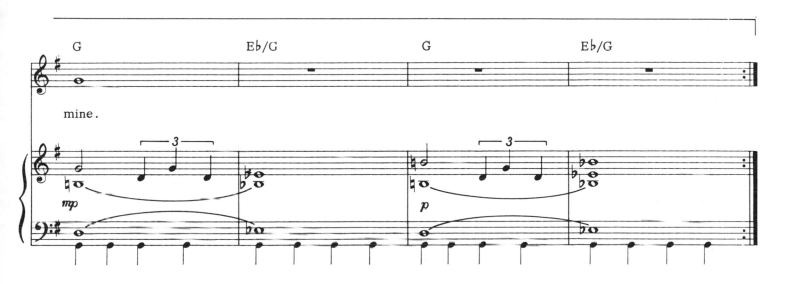

mine.

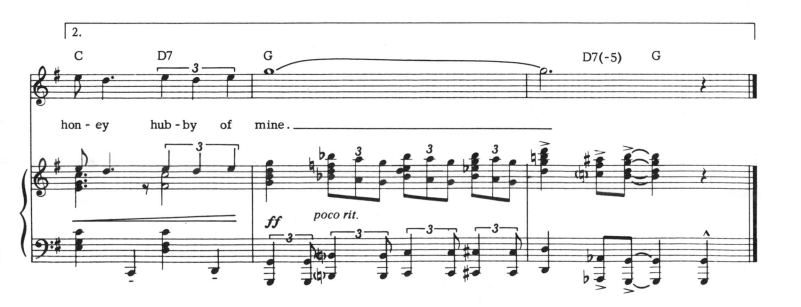

hon - ey hub - by of mine. ___

WHEN YOU'RE GOOD TO MAMA

Words by FRED EBB
Music by JOHN KANDER

Ask an-y of the chick-ies in my pen. They'll tell you I'm the big-gest moth-er hen. I love them all and all of them love me Be-cause the sys-tem works, the sys-tem called re-ci-proc-i-ty!___

*Sung an octave lower

Copyright © 1975 by Unichappell Music Inc. and Kander & Ebb, Inc.
All Rights Administered by Unichappell Music Inc.
International Copyright Secured   All Rights Reserved

CELL BLOCK TANGO

Words by FRED EBB
Music by JOHN KANDER

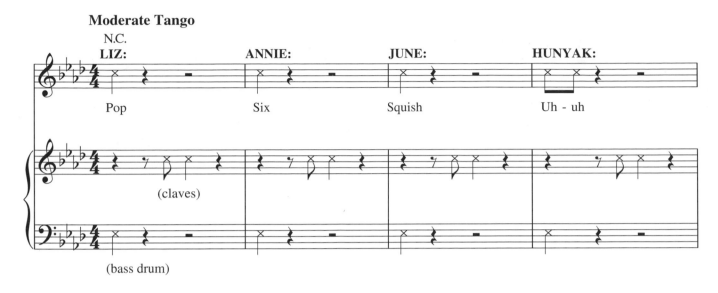

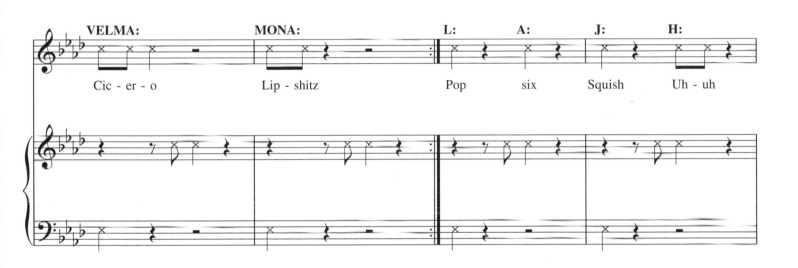

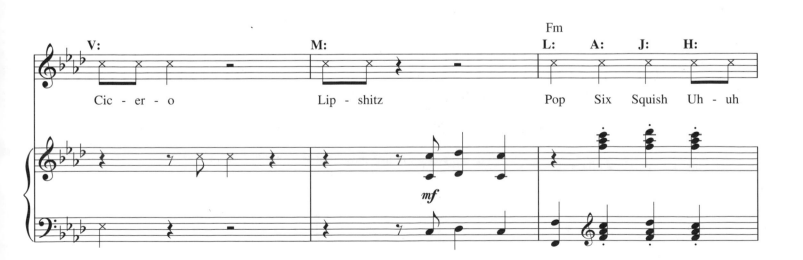

Copyright © 1975 by Unichappell Music Inc. and Kander & Ebb, Inc.
All Rights Administered by Unichappell Music Inc.
International Copyright Secured   All Rights Reserved

Fm   C7+   F   C7+   F   C7+

same.   He had it com - in',   he had it com - in',   he on - ly

F   F7   1

had him - self to blame. ____

LIZ, spoken cue: So I took the shotgun off the wall and fired two warning shots into his head.

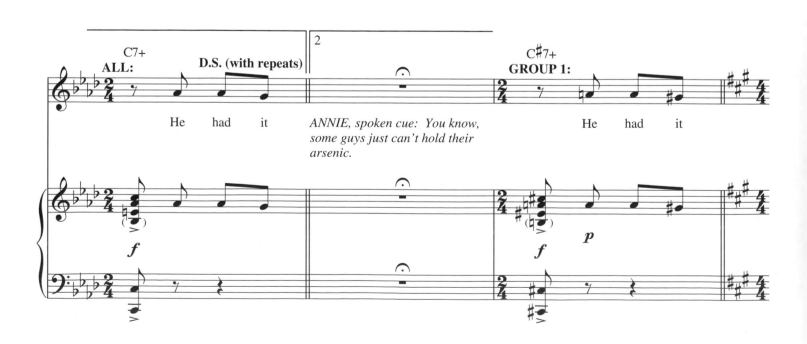

C7+   2   C#7+

ALL: **D.S. (with repeats)**   **GROUP 1:**

He had it   *ANNIE, spoken cue: You know, some guys just can't hold their arsenic.*   He had it

f   f   p

seen it, I bet-cha you would have done the same.

(Hunyak speaks her story)

blame.

If you'd have been there,

if you'd have seen it, I bet - cha

you would have felt the same.

MONA, spoken cue: I guess you could say we broke up because of artistic differences. He saw himself alive and I saw him dead.

ALL:

bum, bum, __ bum, _____ bum, bum, the dirt - y

The dirt - y bum, _____ the dirt - y

ALL I CARE ABOUT

Words by FRED EBB
Music by JOHN KANDER

Copyright © 1975 by Unichappell Music Inc. and Kander & Ebb, Inc.
All Rights Administered by Unichappell Music Inc.
International Copyright Secured   All Rights Reserved

WE BOTH REACHED FOR THE GUN

Words by FRED EBB
Music by JOHN KANDER

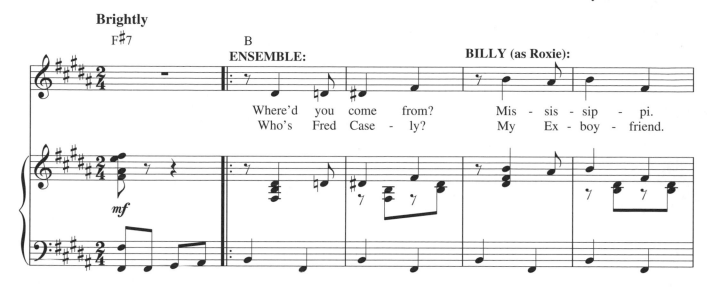

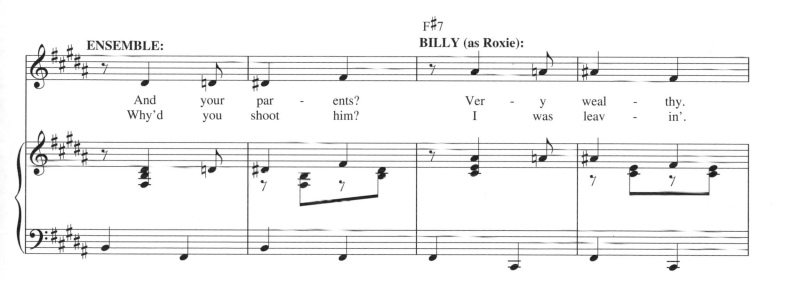

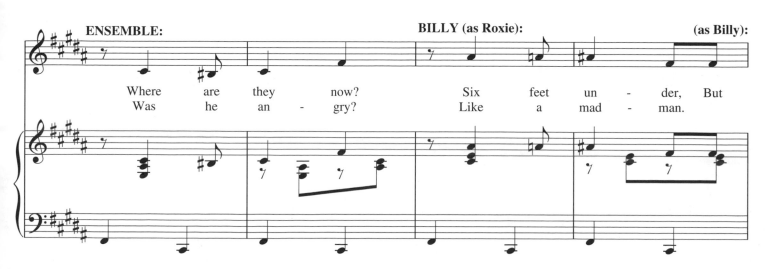

Copyright © 1975 by Unichappell Music Inc. and Kander & Ebb, Inc.
All Rights Administered by Unichappell Music Inc.
International Copyright Secured   All Rights Reserved

F#7 N.C.   B

And he stole my heart a - way, con - vinced me to e - lope one day.

(as Billy):

He had strength and she had none, And yet we both reached for the gun.

1

B   F#7(#9)+   B   F#7(#9)+

(Mary Sunshine speaks)

B   F#7(#9)+   B   F#7(#9)+

2

E   B13

Oh yes, oh yes, oh yes,— we both, oh yes, we both, oh yes,— we both reached for

58

ROXIE

Words by FRED EBB
Music by JOHN KANDER

Copyright © 1974, 1975 by Unichappell Music Inc. and Kander & Ebb, Inc.
All Rights Administered by Unichappell Music Inc.
International Copyright Secured All Rights Reserved

I CAN'T DO IT ALONE

Words by FRED EBB
Music by JOHN KANDER

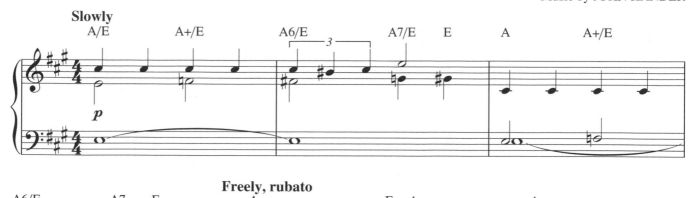

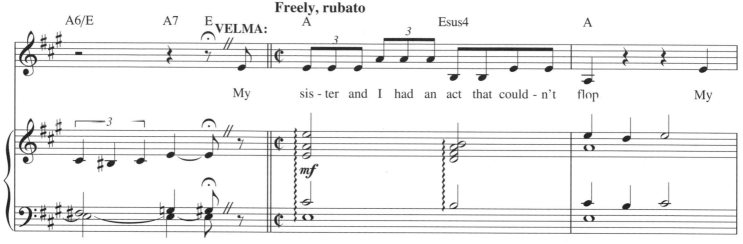

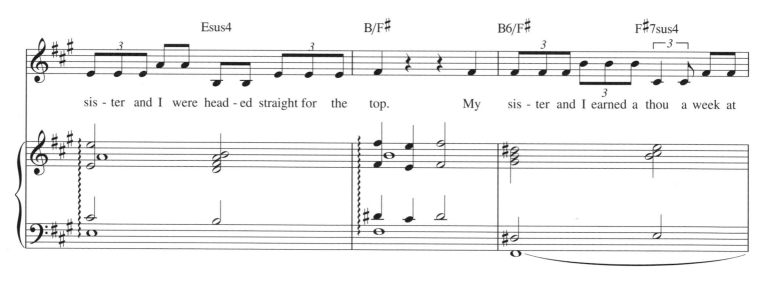

Copyright © 1975 by Unichappell Music Inc. and Kander & Ebb, Inc.
All Rights Administered by Unichappell Music Inc.
International Copyright Secured   All Rights Reserved

sad, of course, but a fact is still a fact.

And now all that re-mains is the re-mains of a

per-fect dou-ble act.

(Spoken:) Watch this! Now, you have to imagine it with two people.

Moderately bright 4

First I'd... *(Choreography)*

Then we'd wow the crowd a - gain ___ when she'd go...

I'd go...

We'd go...

And then those

two - bit John - nies did it up brown ___ to cheer the best at -

trac - tion in town. ___ They near - ly tore the bal - co - ny down. ___

Repeat as needed

(Spoken:) And we'd say, "O.K. boys, we're goin' home, but before we go, here's
a few more parting shots." And this we did in perfect unison.

mp

(percussion)

mf

MISTER CELLOPHANE

Words by FRED EBB
Music by JOHN KANDER

Copyright © 1975 by Unichappell Music Inc. and Kander & Ebb, Inc.
All Rights Administered by Unichappell Music Inc.
International Copyright Secured   All Rights Reserved

RAZZLE DAZZLE

Words by FRED EBB
Music by JOHN KANDER

Copyright © 1974, 1975 by Unichappell Music Inc. and Kander & Ebb, Inc.
All Rights Administered by Unichappell Music Inc.
International Copyright Secured   All Rights Reserved

CLASS

Words by FRED EBB
Music by JOHN KANDER

Copyright © 1975 by Unichappell Music Inc. and Kander & Ebb, Inc.
All Rights Administered by Unichappell Music Inc.
International Copyright Secured   All Rights Reserved

84

NOWADAYS

Words by FRED EBB
Music by JOHN KANDER

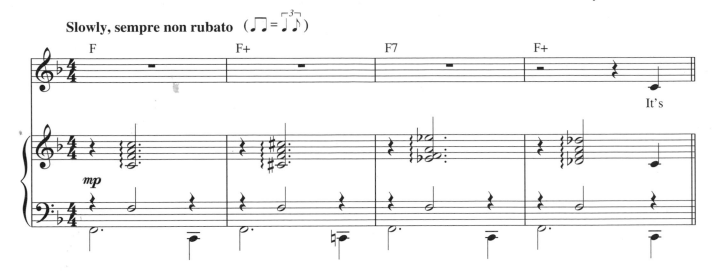

Slowly, sempre non rubato

It's

good, is-n't it? Grand, is-n't it? Great, is-n't it?
men ev-'ry-where, Jazz ev-'ry-where, Booze ev-'ry-where,

Swell, is-n't it? Fun, is-n't it? Now-a-
Life ev-'ry-where, Joy ev-'ry-where,

Copyright © 1975 by Unichappell Music Inc. and Kander & Ebb, Inc.
All Rights Administered by Unichappell Music Inc.
International Copyright Secured   All Rights Reserved

I MOVE ON

from the Motion Picture CHICAGO

Words by FRED EBB
Music by JOHN KANDER

© 2002 KANDER & EBB, INC.
All Rights Administered by WARNER-TAMERLANE PUBLISHING CORP.
All Rights Reserved   Used by Permission